MW00368526

Forever Grateful To You:

Mom

Dad

Andrew

Made in the USA
Coppell, TX
20 May 2022

77994278R00063